easy **GUITAR TAB EDITION**

CLASSIC ACOUSTIC HITS

A No-Nonsense Approach to Playing 10 of Your Favorite Songs

T0040671

How to Access the MP3 Play-Along Tracks on the Enhanced CD

Place the CD in your computer's CD-ROM drive.

Windows: Double-click on My Computer, then right-click on your CD drive icon and select Explore. Open the "Play-Along Tracks" folder to view the MP3 files. Double-click on a file to view it immediately or save it to a folder on your hard drive to view later.

Mac: Double-click on the CD volume named "TNT Song Player" on your desktop. Open the "Play-Along Tracks" folder to view the MP3 files. Double-click on a file to view it immediately or save it to a folder on your hard drive to view later.

About the TNT Feature on the Enhanced CD

You can use the TNT software on your enhanced CD to change keys, loop playback and mute the guitar for play-along. For complete instructions see the **TNT ReadMe.pdf** file on your enhanced CD.

Alfred Publishing Co., Inc.
16320 Roscoe Blvd., Suite 100
P.O. Box 10003
Van Nuys, CA 91410-0003
alfred.com

ISBN-10: 0-7390-5817-7 (Book & CD)
ISBN-13: 978-0-7390-5817-6 (Book & CD)

Cover photographs: Guitarist © Corbis • Lights © Digital Vision

Recordings by Merkin Muffley and His Merrymakers featuring Erick Lynen on vocals.

Contents

DANNY'S SONG

Words and Music by
KENNY LOGGINS

Moderately slow in 2 ♩ = 69

1. Peo - ple__ smile and a
2. Seems as though a
3.4. *See additional lyrics*
5. *Instrumental*

fingerstyle

tell me I'm the luck-y one, and we've just be - gun,__
month a - go I was Be - ta Chi, nev-er got high,

think I'm gon - na have a son.
oh, I was a sor - ry guy.

Danny's Song - 3 - 1

you bring a tear of joy___ to my eyes,___ and tell me___ ev - 'ry -

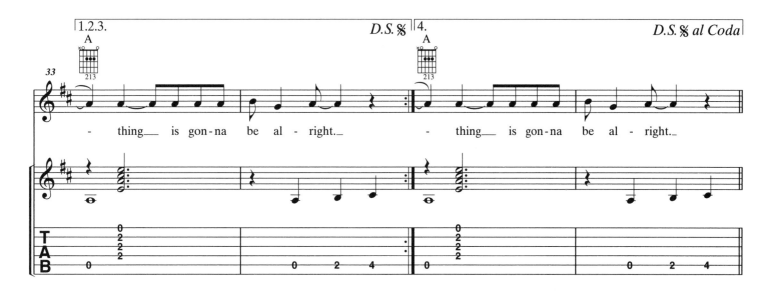

1.2.3.

D.S. 𝄋 4.

D.S. 𝄋 al Coda

- thing___ is gon-na be al - right.___   - thing___ is gon-na be al - right.___

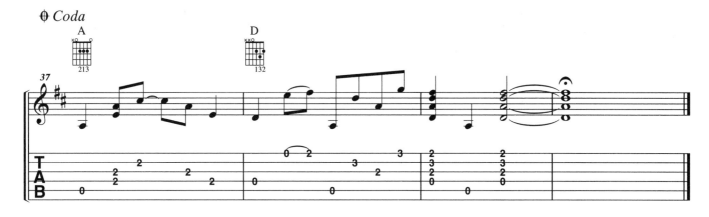

⊕ Coda

Verse 3:
Pisces, Virgo rising is a very good sign,
Strong and kind,
And the little boy is mine.
Now I see a family where there once was none.
Now we've just begun,
Yeah, we're going to fly to the sun.
(To Chorus:)

Verse 4:
Love the girl who holds the world in a paper cup.
Drink it up,
Love her and she'll bring you luck.
And if you find she helps your mind, better take her home,
Don't you live alone, try to earn what lovers own.
(To Chorus:)

BIG YELLOW TAXI

Words and Music by
JONI MITCHELL

Acous. Gtr. in Open E tuning:
⑥ = E ③ = G♯
⑤ = B ② = B
④ = E ① = E

Brightly ♩ = 171

Big Yellow Taxi - 2 - 1

Verse 2:
They took all the trees,
Put 'em in a tree museum.
And they charged the people
A dollar and a half just to see 'em.
(To Chorus:)

Verse 3:
Hey farmer, farmer,
Put away that DDT now.
Give me spots on my apples,
But leave me the birds and the bees,
Please!
(To Chorus:)

Verse 4:
Late last night
I heard the screen door slam.
And a big yellow taxi
Took away my old man.
(To Chorus:)

HOW CAN YOU MEND A BROKEN HEART

Words and Music by
BARRY GIBB and ROBIN GIBB

How Can You Mend a Broken Heart - 2 - 1

INTO THE MYSTIC

To match record key, Capo III

Moderately slow ♩ = 84

Words and Music by
VAN MORRISON

Into the Mystic - 4 - 1

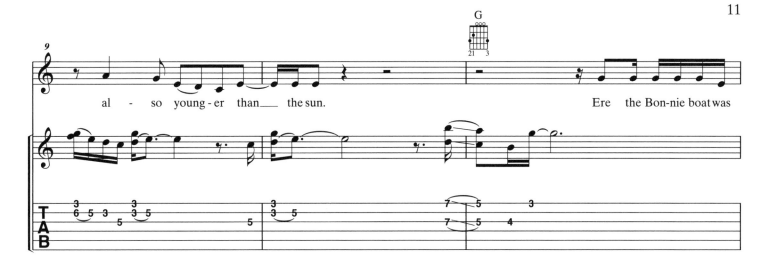

al - so young-er than___ the sun.

Ere the Bon-nie boat was

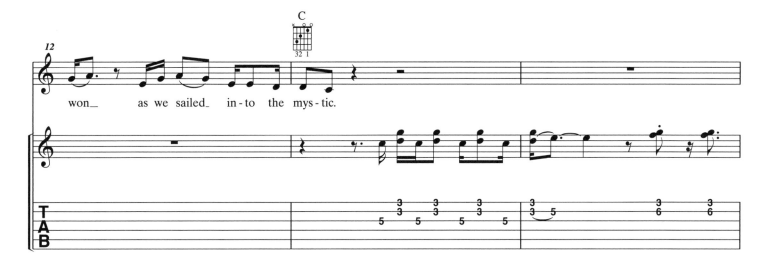

won___ as we sailed___ in-to the mys-tic.

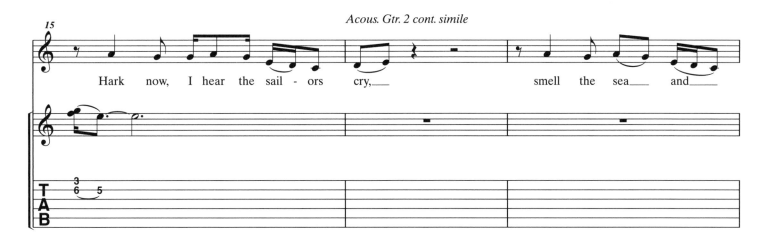

Acous. Gtr. 2 cont. simile

Hark now, I hear the sail - ors cry,___ smell the sea___ and___

feel the sky.___ Let your soul and spir-its fly___ in-to the mys-tic.___

12

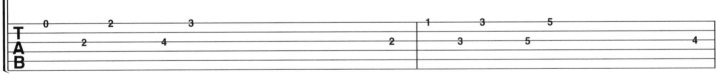

Into the Mystic - 4 - 3

Chorus:

IF YOU COULD READ MY MIND

Words and Music by
GORDON LIGHTFOOT

Capo 2nd fret to match recording.

If You Could Read My Mind - 5 - 1

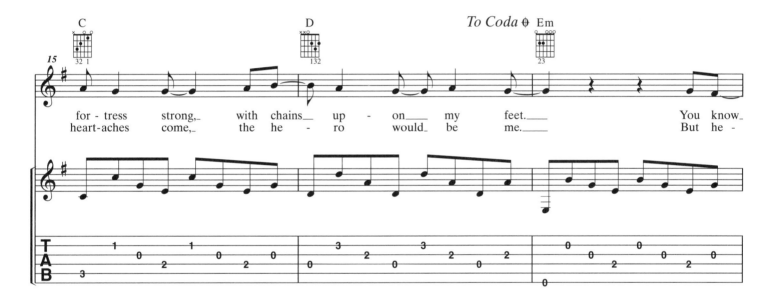

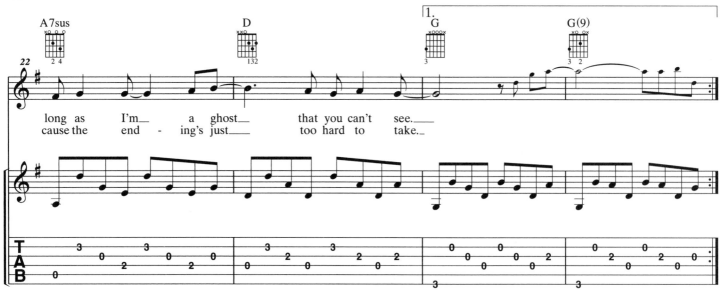

long as I'm__ a ghost__   that you can't   see.__
cause the   end - ing's just__   too hard to   take.__

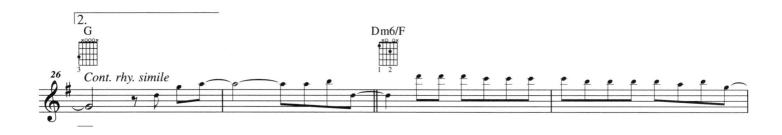

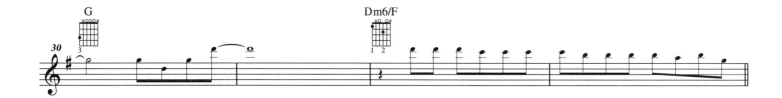

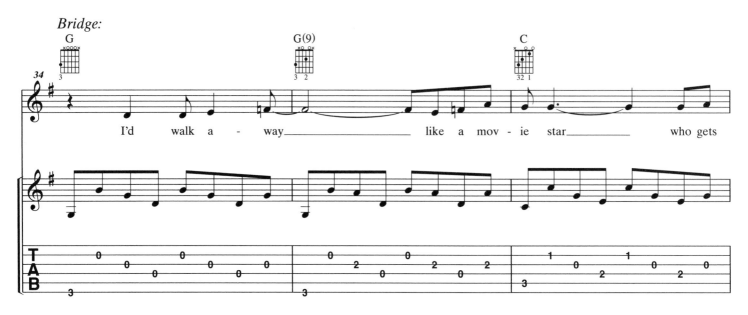

Bridge:

I'd   walk a - way_____   like a mov - ie star_____   who gets

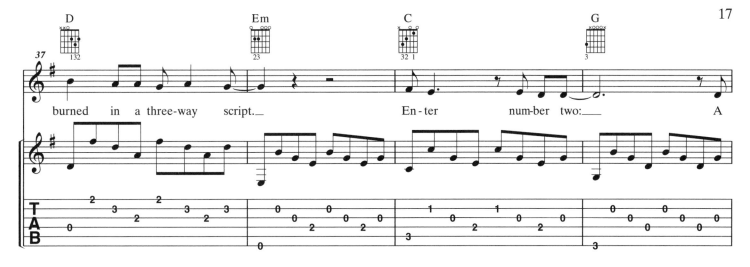

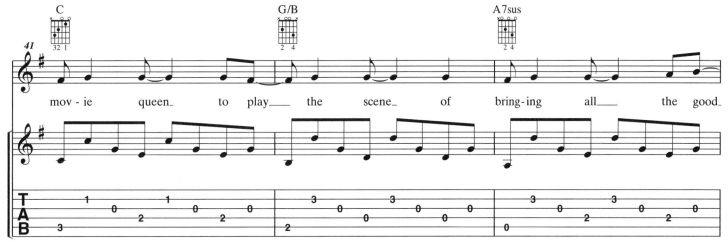

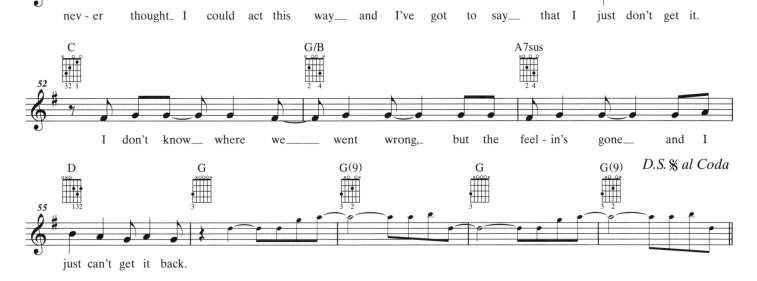

If You Could Read My Mind - 5 - 4

18

MARGARITAVILLE

Moderately ♩=124

Words and Music by
JIMMY BUFFETT

Margaritaville - 3 - 1

20

D.S. % al Coda

Coda

Cont. rhy. simile

Yes, and   some_ peo - ple claim___ that there's_ a

wom - an to blame_____ and I know___   it's my own_ damn_ fault._

Verse 2:
Don't know the reason,
I stayed here all season
With nothing to show but this brand-new tattoo.
But it's a real beauty,
A Mexican cutie,
How it got here I haven't a clue.
(To Chorus:)

Verse 4:
I blew out my flip-flop,
Stepped on a pop-top;
Cut my heel, had to cruise on back home.
But there's booze in the blender,
And soon it will render
That frozen concoction that helps me hang on.
(To Chorus:)

*Verse 3:
Old men in tank tops
Cruising the gift shops
Checking out the chiquitas down by the shore.
They dream about weight loss,
Wish they could be their own boss.
Those three-day vacations become such a bore.

*"Lost" verse (Live version only)

PEACEFUL EASY FEELING

Words and Music by
JACK TEMPCHIN

Verse 2:
And I found out a long time ago
What a woman can do to your soul.
Ah, but she can't take you anyway,
You don't already know how to go.
(To Chorus:)

Verse 3:
Instrumental

Verse 4:
I get this feelin' I may know you
As a lover and a friend.
But this voice keeps whispering in my other ear,
Tells me I may never see you again.
(To Chorus:)

SCARBOROUGH FAIR/CANTICLE

Capo 7th fret to match recording.

Arrangement and Original Countermelody by
PAUL SIMON and ARTHUR GARFUNKEL

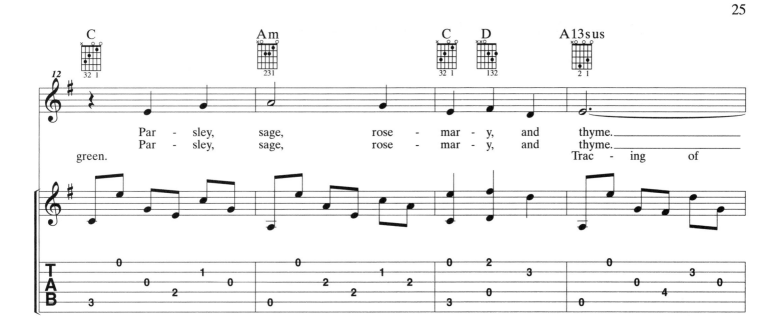

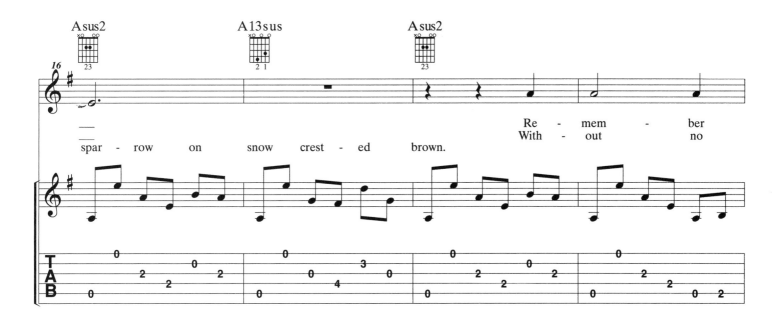

26

Verse 3:
Tell her to find me an acre of land.
On the side of a hill a sprinkling of leaves.
Parsely, sage, rosemary, and thyme.
Washes the grave with silvery tears.
Between the salt water and the sea strand.
A soldier cleans and polishes a gun.
Then she'll be a true love of mine.

Verse 4:
Tell her to reap it in a sickle of leather.
War bellows blazing in scarlet battalions.
Parsley, sage, rosemary, and thyme.
Generals order their soldiers to kill.
And gather it all in a bunch of heather.
And to fight for a cause they've long ago forgotten.
Then she'll be a true love of mine.

VENTURA HIGHWAY

Words and Music by
DEWEY BUNNELL

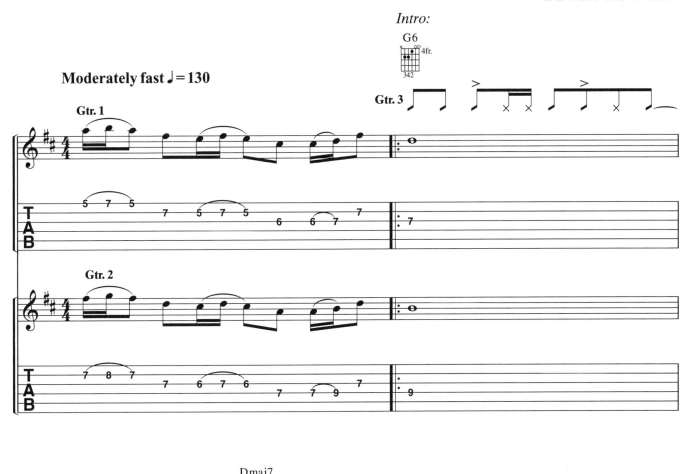

Ventura Highway - 3 - 1

28

WILD HORSES

Words and Music by
MICK JAGGER and KEITH RICHARDS

*Acous. Gtr. is a composite of 6-string and 12-string acous. gtrs.

*Elec. Gtr. simile on repeats.

1. Child - hood liv - ing__ is eas - y to do.__
2. I watched you suf - fer__ a dull_____ ach - ing pain.__
3. I know I dreamed_ you__ a sin_____ and a lie.__

32

Chorus:

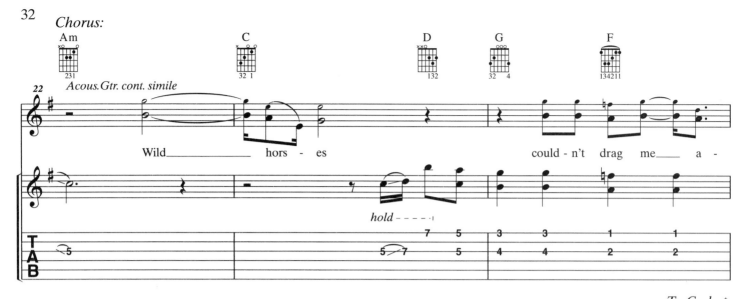

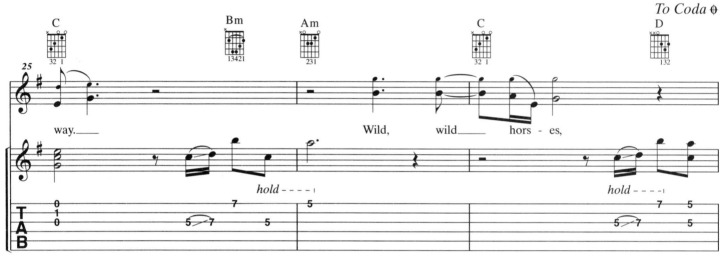

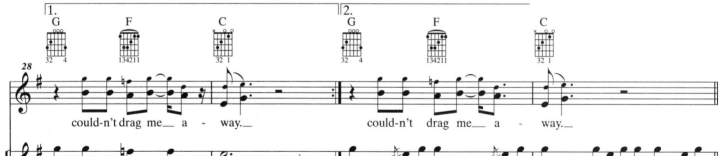

Interlude:

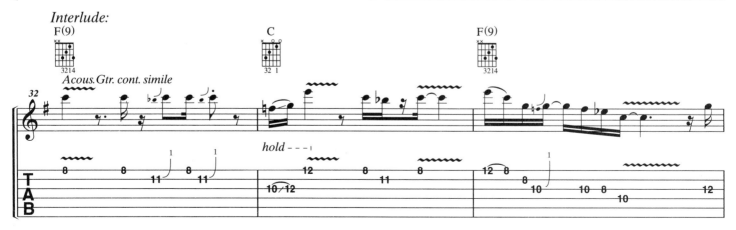

Wild Horses - 4 - 3

TABLATURE EXPLANATION
TAB illustrates the six strings of the guitar.
Notes and chords are indicated by the placement of fret numbers on each string.

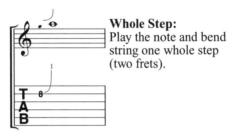

String ⑥, *3rd fret* *String* ①, *12th fret* *A "C" chord* *C chord arpeggiated*
String ③, *13th fret*

BENDING NOTES

Half Step:
Play the note and bend string one half step (one fret).

Whole Step:
Play the note and bend string one whole step (two frets).

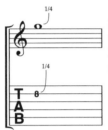

Slight Bend/ Quarter-Tone Bend:
Play the note and bend string sharp.

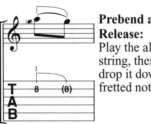

Prebend (Ghost Bend):
Bend to the specified note before the string is plucked.

Prebend and Release:
Play the already-bent string, then immediately drop it down to the fretted note.

Unison Bend:
Play both notes and immediately bend the lower note to the same pitch as the higher note.

Bend and Release:
Play the note and bend to the next pitch, then release to the original note. Only the first note is attacked.

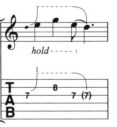

Bends Involving More Than One String:
Play the note and bend the string while playing an additional note on another string. Upon release, relieve the pressure from the additional note allowing the original note to sound alone.

Bends Involving Stationary Notes:
Play both notes and immediately bend the lower note up to pitch. Release bend as indicated.

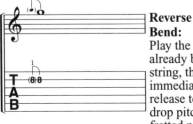

Reverse Bend:
Play the already bent string, then immediately release to drop pitch to fretted note.

Unison Bend:
Play both notes and immediately bend the lower note to the same pitch as the higher note.

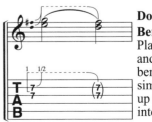

Double Note Bend:
Play both notes and immediately bend both strings simultaneously up the indicated intervals.

ARTICULATIONS

Hammer On (Ascending Slur): Play the lower note, then "hammer" your finger to the higher note. Only the first note is plucked.

Pull Off (Descending Slur): Play the higher note with your first finger already in position on the lower note. Pull your finger off the first note with a strong downward motion that plucks the string—sounding the lower note.

Legato Slide: Play the first note and, keeping pressure applied on the string, slide up to the second note. The diagonal line shows that it is a slide and not a hammer-on or a pull-off.

Muted Strings: A percussive sound is produced by striking the strings while laying the fret hand across them.

Palm Mute: The notes are muted (muffled) by placing the palm of the pick hand lightly on the strings, just in front of the bridge.

Left Hand Hammer: Using only the left hand, hammer on the first note played on each string.

Glissando: Play note and slide in specified direction.

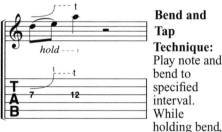

Bend and Tap Technique: Play note and bend to specified interval. While holding bend, tap onto fret indicated with a "t."

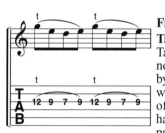

Fretboard Tapping: Tap onto the note indicated by the "t" with a finger of the pick hand, then pull off to the following note held by the fret hand.

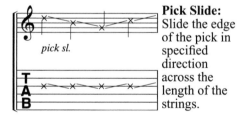

Pick Slide: Slide the edge of the pick in specified direction across the length of the strings.

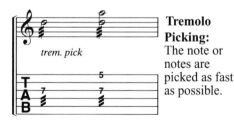

Tremolo Picking: The note or notes are picked as fast as possible.

Trill: Hammer on and pull off consecutively and as fast as possible between the original note and the grace note.

Vibrato: The pitch of a note is varied by a rapid shaking of the fret-hand finger, wrist, and forearm.

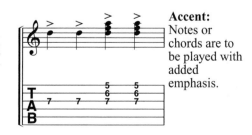

Accent: Notes or chords are to be played with added emphasis.

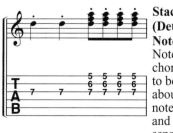

Staccato (Detached Notes): Notes or chords are to be played about half their noted value and with separation.

HARMONICS

harm.   harm.

Natural Harmonic:
A finger of the fret hand lightly touches the string at the note indicated in the TAB and is plucked by the pick producing a bell-like sound called a harmonic.

A.H.

Artificial Harmonic:
Fret the note at the first TAB number, lightly touch the string at the fret indicated in parens (usually 12 frets higher than the fretted note), then pluck the string with an available finger or your pick.

Artificial "Pinch" Harmonic:
A note is fretted as indicated in the TAB, then the picking hand produces a harmonic by squeezing the pick firmly while using the tip of the index finger in the pick attack. If parenthesis are found around the fretted note, it does not sound. No parenthesis means both the fretted note and the A.H. are heard simultaneously.

RHYTHM SLASHES

Strum Marks/ Rhythm Slashes:
Strum with the indicated rhythm pattern. Strum marks can be located above the staff or within the staff.

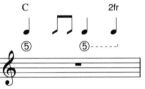

Single Notes with Rhythm Slashes:
Sometimes single notes are incorporated into a strum pattern. The circled number below is the string and the fret number is above.

TREMOLO BAR

trem. bar

Specified Interval:
The pitch of a note or chord is lowered to the specified interval and then return as indicated. The action of the tremolo bar is graphically represented by the peaks and valleys of the diagram.

Unspecified Interval:
The pitch of a note or chord is lowered, usually very dramatically, until the pitch of the string becomes indeterminate.

PICK DIRECTION

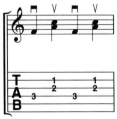

Downstrokes and Upstrokes:
The downstroke is indicated with this symbol (⊓) and the upstroke is indicated with this (V).